YOU NEED THE EYE OF A CERTAIN CLASS IN ORDER TO
PERCEIVE THE SIGNS OF PREVAILING SOCIAL CONDITIONS OF LIFE

— EDWIN HOERNLE

SLIDE
HAVE FUN

YOUR LUCKY DAY

HOT &

I love you
2 BALL'S £3 00
5 BALL'S £5 00
1 WIN LIMIT
DURATION OF FAIR

DS sound
DS sound

MUSHY
WITH
MINT

HOUT
UCE
nal Homemade
HY PEAS
THOUT
AUCE
Mushy Peas £1-50
Large £2-00
lifestyle
Table
Salt
750g℮

THIS IS WHAT
WE LIVE FOR

DYNAMIC

ROMANY
CORAL LEE
VELIFE
SINESS
E GIFT
GINAL
LEE
OR PAIN
READS
ARDS AS
WELL
E STARS

SKIP YEARS OF TRAINING
FEEL THE G FORCE
RIGHT NOW

NOTICE
Health & Safety
Whilst on machine please keep in an upright position and your legs straight

DESTROY THEM WITH
LAZERS

DISCONNECT POWERCORD BEFORE OPENING!
MAAK NETSNOER LOS, ALVORENS TE OPENEN!

ENGLAND

S6 GHC
J.O.H.3.G.

Plush

WINMAU

Place
To
Be

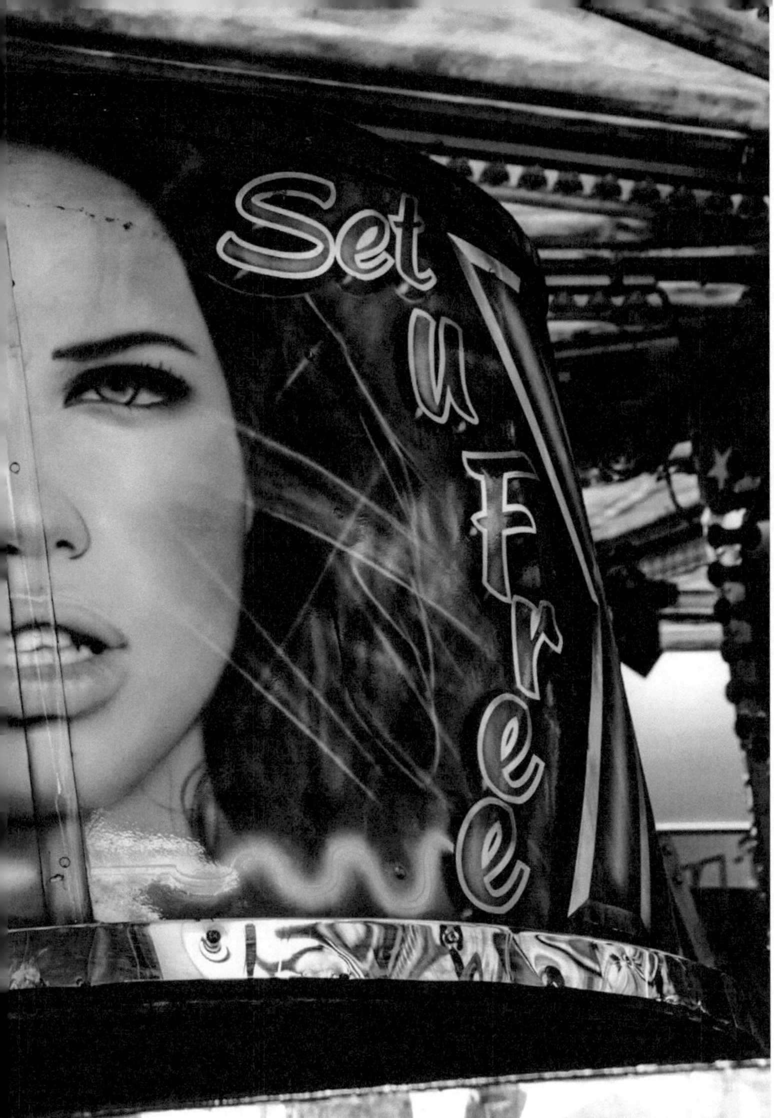
Set
u
Free

START CAR
SEAT BELTS
BOTH ARMS

AFETY ARN SS